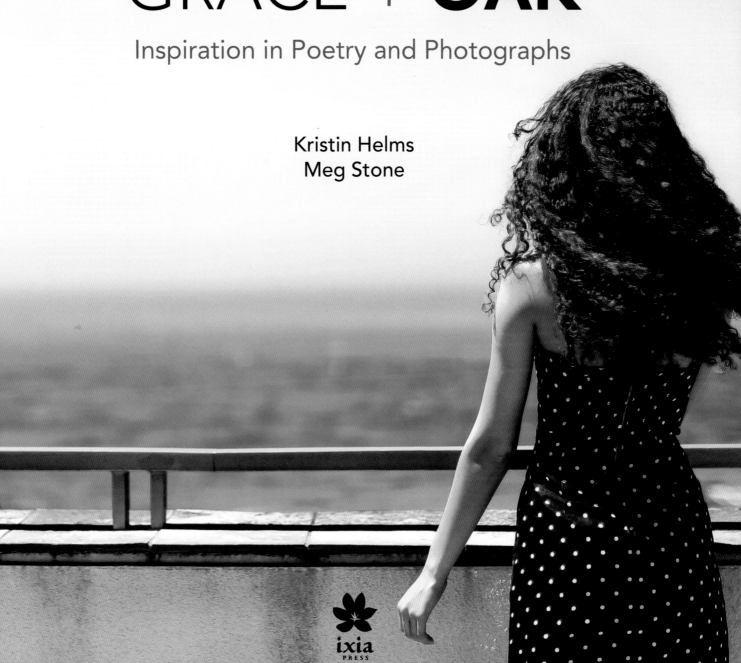

GRACE + **OAK**

Inspiration in Poetry and Photographs

Kristin Helms
Meg Stone

ixia
PRESS

Mineola, New York

Bibliographical Note

Grace + Oak: Inspiration in Poetry and Photographs is a new work,
first published by Ixia Press in 2020.

Library of Congress Cataloging-in-Publication Data

Names: Helms, Kristin, author. | Stone, Meg, author.
Title: Grace + oak : beauty, strength, and inspiration in words and
  photographs / Kristin Helms & Meg Stone.
Other titles: Grace and oak
Description: Mineola, New York : Ixia Press, 2020. | Summary: "Grace
  + Oak is an inspiring collection of over one hundred poems paired
  with fresh and elegant photographs that speak to the creative soul
  that lives in every woman who strives to achieve her dreams. It is
  the first book of its kind to combine moving poetry with stunning
  photography and offer it as a love letter to women pursuing their
  passions. Readers will find themselves moved by the words and
  images to discover their own strength, pursue their dreams, and
  achieve their goals. A beautiful combination of inspirational and
  aspirational, this is a book that women of all ages will want to own
  and share"— Provided by publisher.
Identifiers: LCCN 2019040557 | ISBN 9780486837475 (hardcover)
Subjects: LCGFT: Poetry.
Classification: LCC PS3608.E4656 G73 2020 | DDC 811/.6—dc23
LC record available at https://lccn.loc.gov/2019040557

Ixia Press
An imprint of Dover Publications, Inc.

Manufactured in China by RR Donnelley
83747501
www.doverpublications.com/ixiapress

2 4 6 8 10 9 7 5 3 1

2020

For Mike, Blake, and Gavin—the life and love in my words.

— Kristin Helms

For Mattie, who gives me the courage to fly.

— Meg Stone

FOREWORD

I once read that everything we need to know about life can be learned through nature. I have found this to be less of a platitude and more timeless wisdom.

We are deeply and unquestionably connected with all that is around us. It might be easy to think we are so different, so distinguished, from grass and trees and seasons, but when we look closely, we can see how we are varying expressions of the same form.

If we look at the veins in our wrists, we can recognize that they look like rivers and streams, the kinds of waterways we would trace with our fingers on a map. In fact, all the vessels pumping blood through us resemble nature, like the roots of trees and lightning bolts that crash—all things that deliver vital energy.

Our eyes look like nebulas in the galaxy; our brain looks like the nuts that fall off branches; our skeleton is only fractionally different than that of animals'.

Beyond what is on the surface, we are also very similar just beneath. Our lives often function like seasons. In the same way that the primary goal of nature is to evolve, so, too, are we called to that very purpose. In the manner that stars, when collapsing, are often breaking down into supernovas, so, too, do our lives often fall apart right before our most vital awakening.

What Kristin Helms and Meg Stone have created here is simply that: the awakening. Kristin's encouraging poetry reminds us of our inner power, and Meg's imagery shows us other women who are on this path of emergence.

This is a book for every person who needs to be reminded that there is no time to waste. "Life only promises so many rising suns," Kristin says, and likewise, only so many days for us to wake.

—Brianna Wiest,
  author of *101 Essays That Will Change the Way You Think*

vi   GRACE + **OAK**

PREFACE

Grace + Oak was born from the creative minds of author Kristin Helms and lifestyle and fashion photographer Meg Stone. Kristin and Meg are longtime friends who have always supported and championed each other through pivotal life moments, budding careers, and setting and achieving big goals.

They each launched respective businesses in San Diego and San Francisco, California, following their passions and channeling creativity every step of the way. Above all, Kristin and Meg know firsthand that a creative life is one that requires bounties of grace, an unwavering determination strong as oak, and an enormous amount of inspiration and encouragement along the way.

Both dreamers at heart, Kristin and Meg made this book to fan a flame inside of creative women everywhere: daughters, sisters, mothers, colleagues, friends, and anyone looking for empowerment, beauty, support, and strength while pursuing their dreams.

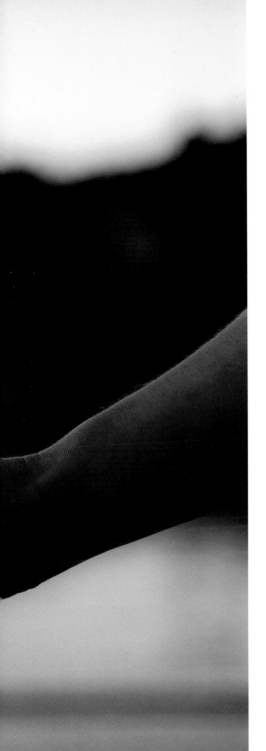

This book is for you,
wild-hearted
soul.

Equal parts grit and *grace.*

Feet planted on the earth,
mind focused on truth and now,
heart beating with stars and future.

Chasing your vision born from dreams of achieving
     something more
     something bigger
     something significant.

Your determination, deep-rooted—strong as *oak.*

When you feel lost,
let this be your moon trail.
When your fire within starts to dim,
let this strike a spark.
When you doubt or fear,
let this remind you of your strength.

Know you're unstoppable because
you
believe in
you.

(We do, too)

xx,

Kristin Helms   *Meg Stone*

What is strength
or endurance
or stability
if not an oak tree
unapologetically living
and growing
in all her wild
glory?

Girl,
you're strong as oak.

All aboard
this bullet train to
everything we've
ever wanted
and worked for
and deserved.
We're charging
loud and proud and strong

Don't you feel this motion? This might?

Come with us.

Magic is mortal,
after all.

Nothing more than
courage and heart,
vitality and conviction.
The belief that you can.

GUESS WHAT?

You can.

Rhythmic steps
in scattered skies.
Shining despite
weather.
Twirling—not for show,
but because
I like to dance.

Freedom.

Art.

This is mine.

So let your
past be.
Acknowledge
what made you—
the demons
and the
stars.
That push and pull
of chaos,
breaking
and shaping
grit and spirit.

Thank it.
Own it.
Set it free.

Take a
moment
and ground
yourself
in this present
moment of
earth and bone
and strength
and know,

it's your time to
rise up.

ALWAYS GROWING,

PUSHING BOUNDARIES,

LEARNING FROM FAILURES.

SUCCEEDING BECAUSE

I allowed myself to grow and fail

ALONG THE WAY.

It starts
as a tiny fleck of a thought.
        A seed.
        A maybe.
        A what-if.
Then that thought
grows and sprouts
upward and outward
through your veins,
and brain,
and heart,
until it consumes
you.
It's chosen
you
to bring it to life.

Oh, the excitement
of a brilliant
idea!

Oh, the task of
growing a forest
from a seed.

And oh, the soul
it takes to
start.

I'm hopeful
and I think
that's the best
we can be sometimes.

Hope that lights
the night like
the North Star.

Hope that paints
watercolors above
a setting sun.

Hope that we've given
our very best
and if it's truly
meant for us,
it will be ours.

Chase joy,

girl, RUN—

like life
only promises
so many
rising suns.
Search for the moon,
swing from the stars,
move, dance, spin
with the earth
and find your happiness,
your light,
in this one, big, beautiful
life.

Open your eyes
with intention
        and gratitude
        and love.
Start your day
in sunlight despite
what skies offer,
then run toward
your purpose
like it's the chase
of your life.

Heart pounding,
muscles quaking,
lungs gasping.

Do you feel it?
LIFE running through you.

It's so good to be alive
and awake
today.

Know This (a Haiku)

May you always know
you hold power to create
any life you want.

Do you want me to say
the road ahead is easy?
It's not.
That everyone will love you?
They won't.
That there are no obstacles?
There are many.
That you'll always make the right decision?
You won't.

Darling, you'll stumble.

But this is what I'll share,
without waver or doubt,

You're unbreakable.

You'll get back up.
You'll learn and do better.
You'll grow courageous
            and fierce
            and unstoppable.

You'll see.

I see
A THUNDER
within you.
A booming
VOICE
building from
your center
like a
storm ready
to unleash
TRUTH.

YOU WILL BE HEARD.

And when the sun
comes up tomorrow,
breathe in this light,
open your eyes
ready to live
this one life
bright.

The earth might shatter
into pieces,
and the sky might
tumble down
from the darkness,
but your reactions
to misfortune
unveil you.

Who are you in the storms?
When the raindrops are so fierce
they pierce
through skin and bone,
reaching soul?

Did you give up at first
strike?
Or did you make your own
shield
and charge forward,
knowing each season passes
just in time?

Keep marching through
this night,
there's clarity with the sun
rise.

Are we alive?
Breathing, yes.
Living? . . .

Stand up on a chair
and sing your favorite song, loud.
Jump into the pool
fully clothed.
Run under the moonlight
in the nude.
Roll down a grass hill
like a child.
Climb a mountain and scream
into the abyss.
Go for a drive with windows
down, music permeating.

Shed your reservations,
lean in to your
wild.

If you do it for show
or applause
or approval,
you'll feed your ego for fleeting seconds,
and deprive your soul of eternal happiness.

So,
do it for you.
Eyes down, heart focused.

Award your spirit,
fan your flame,
expand your mind

in all the ways you need to thrive.

Let authenticity drive you.

Flowers sprouted from her
mind, forming
branches and blooms of
thoughts
      so big,
      so pure,
      so beautiful,
they'd brighten the world
in all the right shades of
happiness.

What if we
synchronized our
movements into one
powerful motion
of hope
and acceptance
and change?

What if we started now?

Find your
center.
The middle place
of your soul that keeps
you balanced and upright—
stable
in these moments of
evolution and change.

It takes core
beliefs and strength
to live life from this foundation
of complete alignment.

So adjust,
level up,
teeter back.

Anchor in peace.

The sky will fall.
The foundation will shake.
Sift the lessons
from the wreckage
like gold from mud.
Treasure these pieces, safe.
Now tools, shields, sparks—
your knowledge,
your strength,
your light.

Maybe
the stars, as we know them,
are a part of us.

Born from us.

Maybe
we finally confronted
the dark,
tired of a life
with no magic.

Maybe
the stars are sparks
that floated up,
hopeful,
from our creative work
here on Earth.
And they were so bright
they lit
the sky—

a twinkling rebellion
and striking contradiction
to the dark.

YES, THE STARS ARE OURS.

She often wondered if
her efforts were going
unseen—lost in the
noise of the world.
But then she realized
her work, her craft,
lit a fire in her soul,
and that's all that really mattered,
and all you can really ask
from a *life well lived.*

And don't forget to
celebrate,
new perspectives disguised
as failures
and wins because of
endurance
and sacrifice.

And the minute.
And the colossal.
And the disasters.
And the gold.

Because you're writing
your journey.
Each step, a landmark.
Each misstep, a lesson.

Because you're unstoppable
and fierce
and worthy
of praise.

There's a truth
woven in your
roots,
so dig down
and trace your
fingers over the
beginning.
Remind yourself
the way you
lived before
judgements
weathered your
branches and rustled
your leaves.

No matter the season,
your roots remain pure.

Your energy is
piercing.

Your mission,
clear.

Don't you see?

The waves and the hills
and the birds and the clouds
and the grass and the trees
all swaying and shifting
because you're here.

Don't break stride now,
we're counting on your
billowing winds moving
boulders and seas.

Courage run
through me.

Power my
spirit and brighten
my view.

These mountains were
made to
strengthen us
so let's climb
and collect
      skills and
        might and
          grit
along this spinning,
unpaved life.

Let's descend the
other side
smarter, stronger,

A KING

having conquered it
all.

◇◇◇◇◇◇◇◇◇◇◇◇◇◇◇◇◇◇◇◇◇◇◇◇◇◇◇◇◇◇◇◇◇◇

She was
vibrant
like the wildflowers,
rooted
like the oak tree,
independent
like the night owl,
bright
like the harvest moon.

Her soul, the
reflection of the world
around her—
courageous and free.

Oh, the triumph the
sea must feel when
its strongest waves
reach the farthest
shores of high tide.

And how humble
it must feel in the low tides—
rewarding beach combers
with treasures
gleaned from rock
bottom trips.

And despite the dark depths
and lonely secrets
the ocean keeps
a continuous, repetitive
motion forward.

Forever on a mission
to take pride in the journey.

Showered in *confidence,*
dressed in *motivation,*
and ready to make this
day *shine.*

Where you've been
is not where you're
going so set free
old stories
like doves released
from a cage made of past
bars and restraints.

Take this pen,
grasp it tight
between your fingers,
and write down
your future.

Make it bright
and bold and
courageous
and fun
and lovely.

Give yourself grace.
Give yourself power.

You have it all to
write and give
yourself.

Toss off your shoes
and roll up your pants.
Let the damp grass
embrace your feet
and learn your
mark.
Walk slowly
toward water,
feeling the earth
soften to mud between
your toes.
Standing at the edge
of the stillness
look down at the
reflection
looking up at you
and tell me
what you see.
Spare me
vanity and shells.

I want to know the
soul in the eyes,
the *waves* that move you,
the *weather* that built you,
the *currents* that brought you here.

How far have you come?
Where are you going?

What's keeping you here?

I HAVE A POCKETFUL OF PIXIE DUST
AND I PLAN ON TOSSING IT
EVERYWHERE THE SUN TOUCHES
AND THE MOON KISSES BECAUSE

WHY NOT SHARE WHAT HAS
BEEN GIVEN TO ME TO ADD
A LITTLE MAGIC TO THIS LIFE?

Allow yourself to unfold,
open layer by layer.
Drink this day
of fresh beginnings
and new moments.
Grow here gorgeous
from the inside shining
in light and warmth
or shade and rain.
Your true, beautiful
soul is not reliant
on something as fickle as
the weather around you.

Watch
the world
shift

once you
realize
you're the orchestrator
and the orchestra
in your own life's
symphony.

There's freedom
and power
in that
music.

Every spring I'm reminded
new beginnings are circular,
second chances, plenty.
The sun does shine, again
and again.

I love a full moon
but I see my reflection
in the crescent.

*An illuminated
sign of hope*
still in the sky.
A work in progress,
growing through the days and
into the nights.

If you lean close enough
she whispers:

Your future is full
and bright.

When life boils
over
and your spirit is
tangled,

    look up to the birds,
    down to the stones,
    left to the sea,
    right to the hills.

There are
miracles
woven
in the ordinary,
beauty
in the details,
inspiration
in simplicity.

It's a weird thing
to put faith
in feathers.
Feathers on wings.
Wings negotiating wind.

Soaring.
Falling.
Gliding.

Faith through it all.

But these are my wings,
my feathers,
my flight.

*And I've never trusted
anything more.*

But understand
this above all:

Everything you touch
      physically or
      mentally or
      spiritually
ripples outward and
circles the earth until
it comes back to you
in later years and gives you
exactly what you gave first.

So give love.
Give truth.
Give kindness.

Give it all,
the best of you.

And if I seem different
it's because

I am.

My
goals and passions
now burn
brighter than my
fears.

I won't stop until
I've lassoed
the sun.

Just watch.

What a sight,
a palm tree
weathering a storm
with lashing winds,
seething skies,
the hiss and sting
of rain.
Electric fire thrown
down like daggers—
highlighting horror,
piercing darkness.

And the palm,
tall and sure
despite whipping leaves
a bending trunk,
fighting still.
ROOTED
despite catastrophe.

Peacefully triumphant,
UNWAVERING.
A symbol
that strength stems from
deep beneath the surface.

But I'm not easily defined
like black and white.
You see, I've painted
a vibrant red paired
with a calming green,
and a warm yellow
next to a chilled blue.
And these colors touch
and blend
in some places
then stand alone,
proud,
in others.
It's me on canvas,
unique and true.

Sometimes complicated and clashing.
Sometimes tidied up, sound.

I've come to realize,
the world needs elaborate
masterpieces like
this.

Elaborate masterpieces like
me.

There's a
boldness
in the way
you talk
about your dreams.

It's in the sure
smile at the edge of your
lips
and the blaring
beam in your
gaze.

You're exuding deep
colors
and intricate
textures.

Just words leaving
your mouth,
but really
brave
plans for a future
you've been painting
all along.

You'll feel an internal
shift
like an eclipse of the
soul,
a wave that washes
over dry sand and
leaves it
glistening and changed.

And you'll know it's
time to
dive
into the possibilities
of your
dreams.

Trust that guiding
current
when it comes for
you.

Get in,
we're headed straight for
everything they said
we couldn't have,
and I just know in my gut,
we'll get there
just in time to
take it all.

When I didn't know where to turn
I faced the sun
and conversed with her rays.
They danced on my face,
warm and vibrant.
I closed my eyes and
listened to the silence
of their embrace.
Worth a million words,
offering grace
and kindness—*acceptance.*
A soft place
for my soul to
land.

Then I understood,
I was never alone.

What if you started now,
inspired in this moment of

nothing special and everything ordinary?
What if you just ran and leaped
into the possibilities you've been
floating around your mind?

I bet you'd fly.

There are wolves
lurking in those
shadows
of the past.

But darling,
you're a flame.

Rising above
the ashes of the
has been.

Brighter,
stronger,
unapologetically
new.

Fiercely lunging
toward the future.

It's yours.

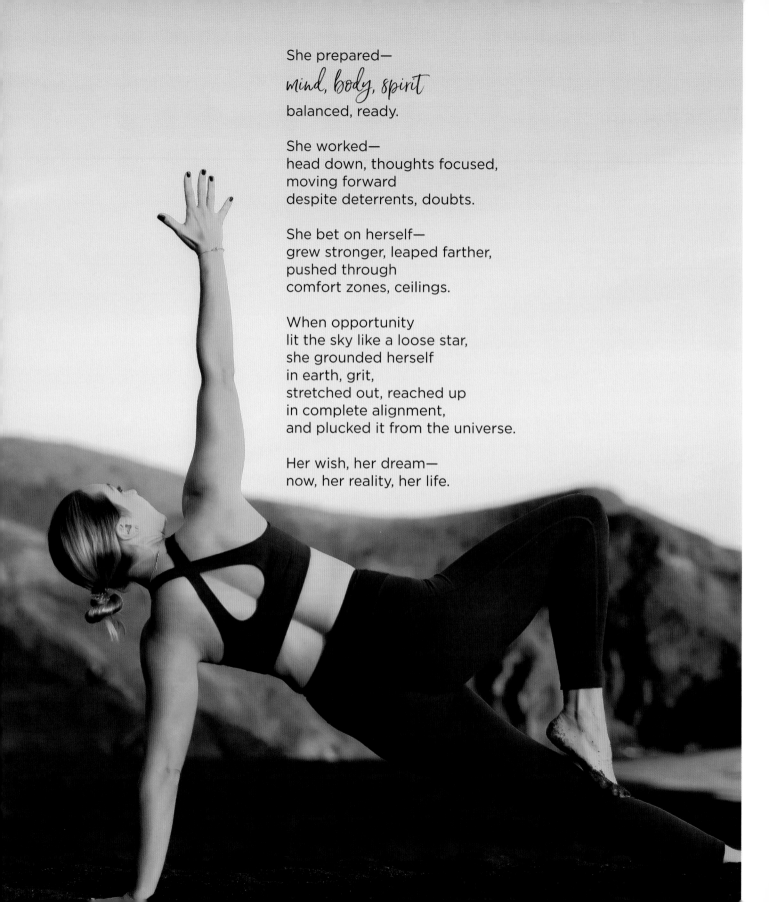

She prepared—
mind, body, spirit
balanced, ready.

She worked—
head down, thoughts focused,
moving forward
despite deterrents, doubts.

She bet on herself—
grew stronger, leaped farther,
pushed through
comfort zones, ceilings.

When opportunity
lit the sky like a loose star,
she grounded herself
in earth, grit,
stretched out, reached up
in complete alignment,
and plucked it from the universe.

Her wish, her dream—
now, her reality, her life.

And don't you feel
like you're just
gaining momentum?
Like this is the turning
point toward
the end goal
you've known
and grown
your whole
life?

That churning in your soul
means you're
in the very moments
that will define
and catapult you.

Look around.
It's all happening now.

Girl,
you glow.
That light is
contagious
so keep
traveling into
the darkest corners—
the ones that have lost faith
in light—
and strike
your match.

Ignite this world
with what you
have inside of
you
and watch the world
set fire
with the brightest, most
magnificent shades of
love and hope.

And I'll tell
you something about
my roots . . .
They've grown deep
and strong
in authentic
truth.

My thoughts
and plans
are pure
and able
to grow
something beautiful
and different
and genuine.

COME LISTEN
to this future.

IT'S NOT THAT THE STRONG
ONES NEVER FACED
THE DARK. IT'S THAT THEY
chose to be the light.

And isn't it extraordinary
that you and me and
every other person
in this universe
is so unique
that we each have
a place—a home
in our own vitality?

Executives
        Musicians
Doctors
        Photographers
Lawyers
        Writers

Aren't we all just
living our art?
What we were called
to do.
Whatever makes us
individually
magnificent
in this very moment in
time.

Life and purpose that moves us
to our highest possible
selves.

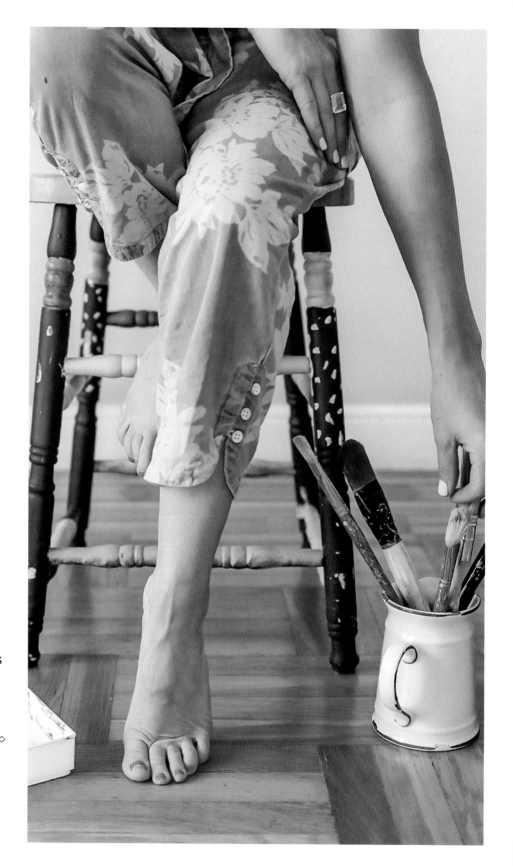

But you see,
my vision was born from
stardust
I swept up
from magical moments
scattered over years
and space,

wishes
I blew out of my
soul toward twinkling
flames
on cakes,

stars
streaked across
the sky, without
apology or explanation,

and spare
pennies,
just mortal carriers
of wishes and luck,
submerged in sparkling
fountains that keep
secrets.

You see,
the universe knows
my dreams.

She floated right past them.

In the deepest shades of night,
up with the wild owls.

Then began again early,
in the clarity
of soft morning light.

Her dedication,
silent and pure.
Her determination,
fierce.

She kept on,
despite obstacle
or circumstance.

She believed.

Her vision,
stronger
than her
fears.

They only paid attention
when she reached
the top.
Then muttered
rootless words
like easy and luck.

With every strand of grace
laced through her soul,
she smiled
then sang truth:

Think only what gives you peace
about your own
affairs.

Tonight I'll sleep sound,
knowing the magic,
born from grit,
I've created with my own
two hands.

In a world of deconstruction,
be a builder
    of spirits,
    and hope
    and action and
    dreams.

Of change
and truth
and progress.

Let's do it together.

I see your
wanderlust
like a wild
owl in search
of answers.

Don't stop this
quest.

You're discovering
meaning and life,
yourself
around corners giving way to
truth.

Did you mistake my
vigor
for a life without
quake?

Remember,
strength
is born from the
cracks.

Passion blazing from the
fire,

grit rising up from the
dust.

And I've settled here,
strong.

Ready for every tomorrow.

I want you to know:

You have everything
it takes inside
of you.

Continue living in this truth.

The first
steps
often feel shaky
as you navigate
new goals.

A new way of living
and thinking.

Allow yourself
time
to create
 momentum,
 rhythm,
 your magic.

It's this
unbalanced,
far from perfect,
obstacle-ridden
journey
that's building
strength
in you.

But you—you're on the
very verge
of *blooming, becoming*
who you really are. You are
a *rare rose, ready*
to reveal pastels, petals
from your *visionary vine* of
promising power.

Lean in
to this spring.

Chasing
dreams with
eyes open,
spirit hopeful,
heart *fierce*.

I had a dream I
was swimming in
a black sea,
but it wasn't water,
it was sky.
And I was barely floating
between falls
and I was desperately reaching
between fumbles.
But then I opened
my eyes and saw
the stars because of the dark
and they burned
a message into my soul
so bright
I'll forever see,
so powerful
I'll forever abide . . .

Keep going.

Some days
require champagne
on rooftops
simply because
tomorrow is
a gamble. But what
we know for sure,
what we have now,
is this moment—
a tiny celebration of
breathing in this
sunlight.

She wore her
confidence like
a humble crown
made from wild
flowers and twigs,
beautiful from the
earth. Grounded in

her own becoming.

When she *moves*
the world feels it
without realizing.
Her energy hums over
mountain tops,
skips across rivers,
runs wild in brush fields and
dives deep into oceans.
The world made better by the
kindness in her vibrations.

Throw
your anchor
overboard and
ground
yourself in the
sparkling
rocks below.

Plant yourself
in this depth-reaching
sunshine
where happiness
floats from your
lashes and your heart
beats steady and strong in
velvet waves of salt.

Your space.
Your time.
Your life.

Stretch your limbs,
swim toward
the light
in this charming sea
of freedom.

She didn't walk
nor run
toward her goals.

She danced.

Twirling, moving,
grooving
into the rhythms
that made her feel
alive and free.

Loved.

It was impossible
not to watch,
even harder not to
join.

She always found
fairytale endings
boring. Everything
tied up in a neat bow,
forevermore.

She'd trade in such
fantasies in exchange for
waking
every morning
in love with herself
and her mission
and her truth
and her grace.

She needed substance and
challenges—reasons for
growth and perspective.

Reasons for discovery and
change.

Reasons to breathe.

She found inspiration
in the simple grace of falling
leaves from aged
oak trees,
cotton clouds gliding,
morphing across
indigo skies,
the promising smell
of the wind
preluding rain,
and other humans who
revel in these
types of wonders
too.

She didn't fear
life's fires—
she grew up
dancing through
flames.
Now, the ashes
swept and sorted,
a piece of her
somehow grateful for
the scars, endurance—
HER STRENGTH.

Dear hurricanes of nature or flesh,

Good luck disrupting
these iron roots.
They've grown courageous and
stubborn in a foundation of
light and love and strength.

I promise, if
you knock me down,
I'll stand back up.

WATCH THE ROOM
LIGHT UP WHEN YOUR
AUTHENTIC SELF
shines true
AND BRIGHT.

It's that rhapsody you play
over and over in your head.
It originated in your lungs—
          your very breath,
and circulated through your veins,
      by way of your heart,
outstretching to your limbs,
lingering forevermore
in your mind.

Music and verse,
your
song that moves
you
in patterns and whim,
through circumstance and plans.

So turn it up loud,
charge the earth's edges until
you find a tune that
strikes harmony
with your own
soul.
Then play it over
and over and
over.
Again.

Don't worry about being
BEST or FIRST or MOST.

Worry about losing
authenticity.
Worry about losing
passion.
Worry about losing
yourself.

Rest peaceful and proud in your
novel presence.
That's where you shine
true.

You are

Big. Huge. Important.

Unique. Kind. True.

Stop allowing space for
anything that makes you feel small
or not exactly like
you.

I'm not doing it for glory
nor award.
It's much bigger than ego.
Much bigger than me.
This mission is for every woman
with or without a voice.

I'm doing it because it's right
and needed
and time.

If you try to put me in a white box
I'll push down the walls,
one by one,
dip my feet in bright colors of paint,
then skate across the page with no edges,
or pattern.
I'll glide right past expectations
and show you everything
I am that you didn't expect.

Look at this colorful soul,
vibrant and worthy of everything
that doesn't belong inside of a
white box.

And it's OK to be
many things
all at once.

Don't apologize for
contradicting pieces—
you are a complex
soul that's allowed to
encompass everything
you are.

Intricate authenticity shines through
you, *proud.*

Don't cry over
a broken crown.
You never needed that to
prove power.
We see strength
in your eyes, motions, and soul.
Unshakable, unbreakable
vigor grows in your heart
and manifests from your being.

It's this boldness within you
that shines through,
bright.

THE STARS ARE OLD FRIENDS, AFTER ALL.
ALWAYS THERE TO WELCOME
new dreams.

Because I've worked
too hard for this moment.

Because I've traveled
too far—along twisting, snaking,
roads.

Because this idea was
created in my mind and
born in my soul
and it's this kind of mortal
magic the world needs
now.

Because I've used everything
I was
and am
and will be.

Because I was told
I can't,
over and over
again.

Because I believe in
myself.

Because I can.

She left stardust in
her steps
and springtime in
her wake.

Following her lead was
effortless and inspiring—
a season of soulful work
that changed spirits and
lives.

Lovely. Honest. Kind.

She was
A WILD CHILD FROLICKING THROUGH UNRULY BLOOMS,

She is
A DREAMER SWINGING ON BURNING STARS IN BLACK SKIES,

She'll be
AN UNWAVERING LIGHT THROUGH SEASONS OF SUN OR STORM.

I've crawled through the night,
slipped down atmospheric clouds of dust,
teetering on edges of sharp
stars, galaxies away from where I
started—swimming breathless.

When my eyes opened gently and
my feet felt ground, I thought I
landed on the moon but then
saw life in green leaves
and warm eyes,
life in me.
Rocketman turned earth child,
breathing finally, settled
purposefully back living here
in daylight.

Good morning.

These arms like steel,
lifting you higher.

Keep going.

This love like a net,
in case you fall.

I'm right here.

These words like wings,
whispering courage.

You can fly.

Pay attention
to winds
that bring
even slight
shifts in
moods, rhythms—
atmospheric alternatives.
These are
your winds.
This is
your chance
to lean
into change,
find your
new beat,
and grow

right here,
right now.

It's at the
very edge
of the
steepest cliff—
heart pounding,
legs shaking—
where she found
her lion
strength
and decided, right then—

She would survive.
She would repair.
She would thrive.

So she did.

Let your dreams open
a parachute in
your life.
The *saving grace*
that keeps your soul
alive and hopeful,
afloat.
Even when you can't see the ground.

I've found it—
my ability to believe in myself.
I knew I had tucked it away for a
glorious, beautiful day
like today.

Yes, today is *the perfect day to start believing*
in something as wonderful and capable
and momentous
as me.

Maybe it's the
angle of the
sun piercing through
shifting clouds,
or curious shadows
brightened by mystic
moonlight.
All I know is
I've seen magic now.
Something just outside
our calculated
control.

Alchemy woven
into humanity.

Beautiful, fascinating, real.

Don't come to me with
your judgments, those belong
to you.
Haven't you been judged a
thousand times over?
What good is judgment, anyway?
Looking for the thorns before noticing the rose?
Take me as I am, but please, I beg of you, take the whole me.
The parts buried beneath
wear and face.

Look into my eyes, *my soul lives there*.

In fact, let's lock eyes and hold a silent truce — just two authentic spirits
meeting
for the first time—our truths on display.
Mere mortals, after all, just trying to
make it out alive.

In the clarity
of early morning
light,
the past washes out to
sea,
the future dances along the
horizon,
and everything is possible
now.

And when you get stuck somewhere
in this big, consuming world,
go home.

To your first childhood house,
where memories began and
souls formed from scratch.

Mentally walk
through the rooms,
smell the nostalgia.
Rewind your life to those
first moments of innocence
and truth.

Stay for a while.

Flip through the pages of your history,
the key to your spirit,
the answers to why you dance to this beat.

Move forward, grounded
in your truest self.

She smiled and danced
as if nothing had
ever derailed her vision
or weighed on her soul.
Her spirit—
too strong, too beautiful—
to be harnessed by
something as temporary
as the dark.

Write it down.
Tattoo it on your heart.
Sew it on your sleeve.
Sing it in your dreams.
Hear it echo through your
mind.

It's part of you.
Time to bring it to
life.

START NOW.

AND IF YOU NEED ME,
I'LL BE IN A FIELD OF DAISIES
CHASING MY DREAMS
BY WAY OF MOONLIGHT, DANCING
TO THE DRUMS OF THE CRICKETS
AND THE CHORUS OF THE OWLS.
My wild heart belongs
HERE WHERE I FEEL ALIVE
AND FREE TO BE
COMPLETELY ME.

Some days will derail
and you'll be forced
to feel every bump
charging forward with
no paved path.

But if you slow down
and look close,
there are *wildflowers*
blooming only for those
brave enough to continue
off course.

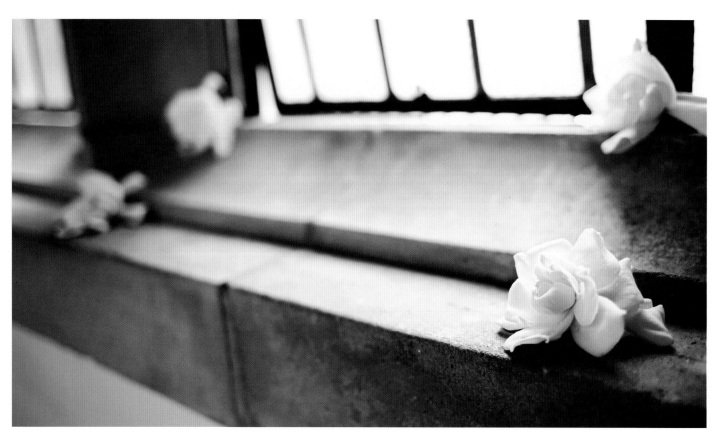

Be so rooted in
your truth that even if
they chop you down,
you'll grow
again.

Stronger this time.

GRACE woven between the edges,
Illuminated by an internal flame,
Realizing strength born from
Love and truth.

Passionate and rooted like the
OAK tree flourishing with
Wonder and determination,
Enriching every space her light touches while
Reaching new heights to spread change.

I believe in you
and your ability to grow a field
of wildflowers from a single seed.

I believe in you
and your spirit to spread soft light
throughout the darkest caves.

I believe in you
to bridle your strength and steer
others in the direction toward success.

I believe in you
and your vision to create
something big and meaningful.

I believe in you
in everything you do.

I AM PERFECT AS
I AM.
EVOLVING, GROWING WITH
EACH BREATH.
PERFECTLY IMPERFECT WITH
EVERY STEP.
IT FEELS *nice to live* IN
THIS TRUTH.

Have you lost your
way somewhere between
the sun and the moon?
Stuck in a cloud of gray
that doesn't illuminate a
a clear direction.

Take this match—
strike a spark
and ignite a flame
again in your spirit
and your step
and your mind,
so you'll always light
and guide your own
journey forward.

Brain:
I guess this must be
the part where I defy
odds and take flight.
When I overcome.
But I'm a mere mortal.
Nothing more than bones
and flesh.

Heart and Soul:
We'll take it from here.

Realize,
no matter how small
you may feel,
the world sways
and bends
when you move.

So, take off—
girl, soar!

We need this
flight,
this change.

You will need to
rest,
repair,
try again.

Don't mistake pit stops
for failure.
These are indicators of
progress and growth
that make way for
energy and strength to
continue and succeed.

It's slight
but finite,
that tidal shift
in your
heart.
There's no going
back
against the currents
of your soul,
so hold fast
to this wave
of change
and *steady yourself*
on this freedom
ride.

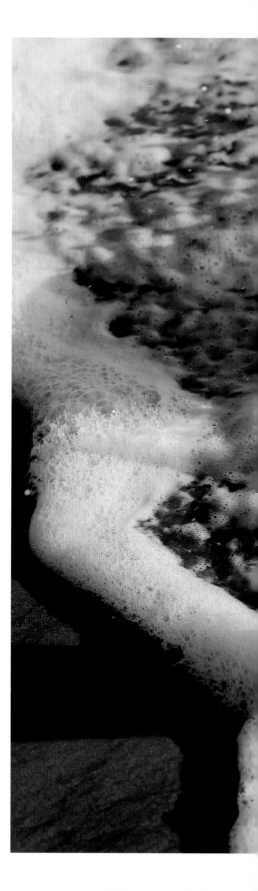

This is all you need to know
about her:

She never stopped
dreaming,
come age or achievement.
As long as there was
life to live, there were
new mountains to charge.

Her adventure burned bright,
a mission with no end.

She just kept
breathing,
practicing gratitude,
speaking kindness.

Living an authentic
life was simple
when she stuck
to the basics of
love and truth.

Watch your boundaries
crumble and fall
as you face new
fears.
Someone like you
is not meant to be boxed in
so keep challenging yourself
and witness the internal growth
that comes from stepping past
comfort zones.

It's lovely out here.

AND WHEN THE PATH GROWS DARK,
SHARE SUN RAYS FROM YOUR SMILE,
LOVE AND KINDNESS FROM YOUR WORDS,
COMFORT FROM YOUR PRESENCE.
THEN WATCH THE UNIVERSE
MIRROR THESE GESTURES
back to you.

She has that
wild heart,
always reaching for
the sun
despite
roots or distance.
That kind of soul
captures the
light.

I'm proud
of who I've become
despite the tangles
of the past.
I've unraveled them
in my lungs,
ironed them out
in my heart,
smoothed the sharp edges
in my mind.

Still a part of me—always,
but now deprived of power
and webs and mess.

Clean lines, clear eyes, pure soul—
I live here now.

She is equal parts
confidence and humility,
strength and compassion,
wild and grace.
It's the balance in her soul and
harmony in her being that
makes her *shine brighter*
than the rest.

Her dreams
were so loud
the stars
paid attention.

Allow each new breath
the opportunity to float
into the universe and offer
kind words,
bold actions,
wings of strength,
a courageous heart . . .

Pieces of you
scattered and planted,
ready to grow
love.

Seconds, minutes, hours
pass without pause.
The world turns like a never
ending record.

Who's choosing the songs?

We charge forward trying to make
it all count. Trying to live in the tiny
moments of space. Trying to hold
on to past moments in time.

It's a *delicate dance* to
cherish the old,
live the now,
learn the new.

But it's getting easier—
more graceful—
with time and
tempo.

I SET IT FREE—
GUILT, SELF-DOUBT, NEGATIVITY.
FLY, FLY, FLY! BE GONE.
YOUR HOME IS NO LONGER HERE WITH ME.

I've decided to let the light in.

Ticking clocks
have a way of
setting expected
rhythms
for our lives.
Stories already written.
But I've never
been a fan of
limits
nor someone else
writing my journey.
So, I'll move,
    unexpectedly,
    unapologetically,
    truly,
to the beats of
my own breath,
on my own time.

Inhaling freedom—tick.
    Exhaling expectations—tock.

Carry on,
Queen,
stay this sunshine course.

The kingdom you're building
shines from within
and you're doing it all with
dignity and grace.

Nothing more from me other than
to say:

Thank you for bringing the light.

And in the stillness
of days spent in mirrors of
mind and reflection,
she felt her
lungs inhale pieces
of present,
exhale fractures and
thorns,
and clear space
for *new blooms*
of intentions.

It's amazing how you can often
feel the very beginning of something not yet defined.
The slightest shift in the universe sends waves of
energy that gain momentum over time and space.

Intuition, maybe. Eagerness, maybe.

All I know is that I feel this change like the
warmest spring after the fiercest winter.
The frost melting into the earth, the birds chirping with conviction.

Don't you know this in your bones?
We're on the brink of something magnificent.

Take a closer
look at my courage.

Built from the broken
moments that crushed
then built
me.
My strength,
born from the shattered
fragments of past
and mended with
a sharp determination to
survive,
        and thrive.

And I've grown
        oh, how I've grown
into a soul who
does whatever it takes.

See, this courage—
my power, my shield—
is me.

Seize this
moment.

It's yours.

Grab these
reigns.

They're yours.

Head off into the sunset
of your wildest dreams.

It's all for you.
Made from you.
Designed by you.

So goodbye, farewell.

Don't look back only
straight into
the reality of everything
ahead on that horizon.

It's waiting for you.

And one day
she realized
that *She*
was the happy
she'd been
searching for in all
the wrong moments,
places and people.
And she tapped into
that internal joy
and watched wildflowers
bloom around her
in every direction
for miles and
miles
without end.

And when you
look into her
eyes, you have no
choice but to
hold your breath and
dive into a
sparkling
sea of intriguing
depths.
Waves and diamonds,
        treasure and salt.

Just before the dark,
in the whispers of light
when souls glow,
she set her intentions free
on swirls of delicate winds,
watched them fold and tuck
into secret pockets of
universe and space,
and she knew without logic—
this was the start of something
extraordinary.

I see the parts of you
that haven't appeared
at the surface.
You've not yet witnessed
your own strength and power
to challenge evil,
spread truth,
and become
the leader that you are.

It's in your bones.

IF THE OPTION IS TO
FOLD
OR
FLY,
DON'T FORGET,
YOU WERE BORN WITH
soul wings.

Darling, know
your power.

Like the moon
shifting tides,
or the stars burning
through black
skies,
or the sea
shaping
coasts.

You're beautifully capable.

NEW BEGINNINGS START WITH ENDINGS SO

CLOSE IT UP,
    LOCK IT DOWN,
        SET IT FREE.

TAKE YOUR FIRST STEPS TOWARD THAT
FLICKERING SKY —
THE DAWN OF A NEW
DAY.

ACKNOWLEDGMENTS

Creating this book was a labor of love fueled by inspiring collaborations. There are so many fierce, talented, amazing women we want to thank for helping bring it to life.

First, our literary agent, Jill Marsal, who saw something special in our pitch and sample pages and charged forward in finding us the perfect publisher. She found us a great home with Ixia Press, and we're all holding this book because of her big efforts in the beginning, when *Grace + Oak* was simply a proposal.

Fiona Hallowell, our California sister representing in New York, thank you! From our first kickoff call, we knew we were in terrific hands with her as our editor. We had the best collaborative experience, and we are forever grateful for her believing in us and this project from start to finish. Also, a huge thank-you to the whole team at Dover Publications (publisher, editors, designers, marketing). It's been a pleasure working with such a creative and capable staff.

To the friends and strangers (now friends) who agreed to be photographed, thank you for your time and effort. We know many of you are not models by trade and sincerely appreciate your courage to step in front of Meg's camera. You women are the embodiment of beauty and strength, *Grace + Oak*.

Thank you to Brianna Wiest for lending us her time and talent by writing an inspiring foreword. We love her wise, empowering prose and are thrilled to have her words as part of the book.

Lastly, thank *you*. This project was never really ours; it's always been yours. Thank you for reading, dreaming, believing, growing, working, achieving right along with us. Let's all continue lifting each other higher.

ABOUT THE AUTHORS

BRITTANY SZABO PHOTOGRAPHY

KRISTIN HELMS is an author and entrepreneur based in San Diego, California, where she lives with her husband and two young children. Her first nonfiction book, *From Boardroom to Baby*, encourages new moms to find grace, strength, and new self-discovery throughout motherhood and provides insights on how to successfully launch a business from home.

Kristin's soulful prose and inspiring thoughts have been published in *PopSugar*, *Literary Mama*, *Home & Garden Magazine*, *Motherly*, and *The Huffington Post*. Her writing has been described as "encouraging," "refreshing," and "magic with words."

As an entrepreneur, Kristin founded and sold the popular parenting website for moms, *Tribe Magazine*, and has since launched a new brand for the dreamers, Verse + Vine.

BRITTANY SZABO PHOTOGRAPHY

MEG STONE is a fashion and lifestyle photographer based in the San Francisco Bay Area where she works with lifestyle brands and fashion influencers to create elevated, scroll-stopping images that attract and inspire the modern woman. Her fresh and sophisticated images have been featured in publications such as *Elle Spain*, *Southern Living Magazine*, *Glitter Guide*, and *The Zoe Report*.

With a passion for entrepreneurship and creativity, Meg left the security of a nine-to-five career in 2014 to pursue her photography dreams. Self-taught and motivated by a pure love for the art, her natural affinity for fashion led her to build a clientele of fashion and lifestyle brands, with the majority being women-owned businesses.

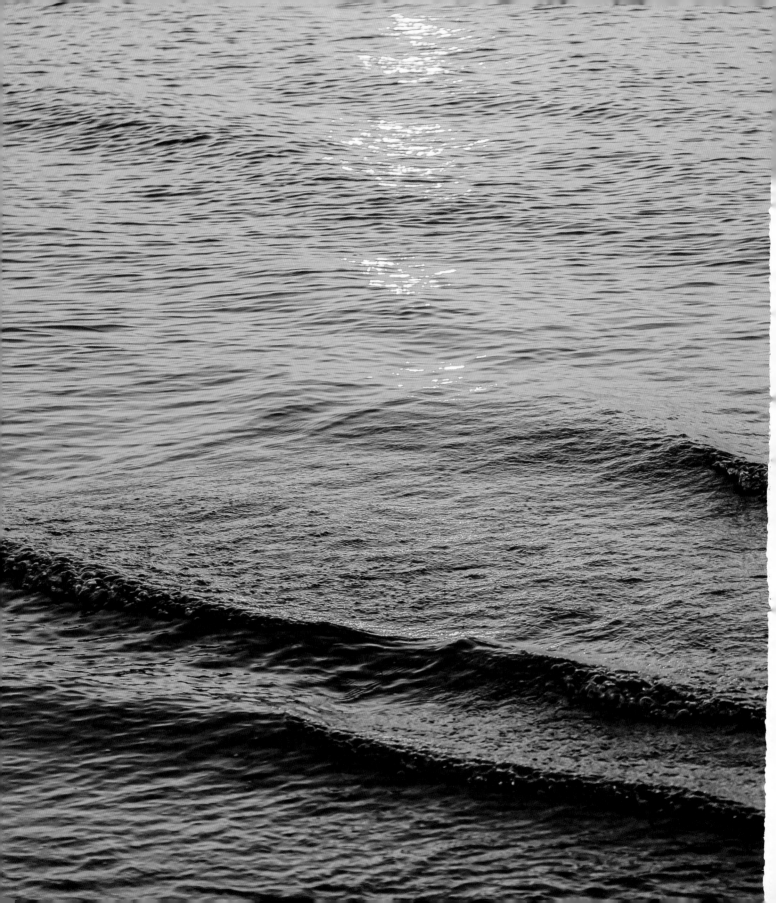